Yellow Umbrella Books are published by Capstone Press
151 Good Counsel Drive, P.O. Box 669, Mankato, Minnesota 56002
http://www.capstone-press.com

Library of Congress Cataloging-in-Publication Data
Ecker, Debbie.
    People work/by Debbie Ecker.
    p. cm.
    Includes index.
    ISBN 0-7368-0740-3
    1. Occupations—Juvenile literature. 2. Work—Juvenile literature. [1. Occupations.
2. Work.] I. Title.
HF5381.2. E25   2001
331.7'02—dc21   00-036481

    Summary: Describes why people work and a variety of occupations.

Editorial Credits:
Susan Evento, Managing Editor/Product Development; Elizabeth Jaffe, Senior Editor;
    Charles Hunt, Designer; Kimberly Danger and Heidi Schoof, Photo Researchers

Photo Credits:
Cover: (clockwise from left) Jim West, Photo Network/Esbin-Anderson, Photo
Network/Bachmann, Visuals Unlimited/Nancy P. Alexander; Title Page: Photri-Microstock
(top left), Index Stock Imagery (bottom left), International Stock/Bill Stanton (top right), Photo
Network/Bachmann (bottom right); Page 2: Visuals Unlimited/Mark E. Gibson (top left),
Leslie O' Shaughnessy (bottom left), Index Stock Imagery (right); Page 3: International
Stock/Mark Bolster (left), Bruce Byers/FPG International LLC (right); Page 4: Photo
Network/Jeff Greenberg; Page 5: International Stock/Scott Barrow; Page 6: Kent & Donna
Dannen; Page 7: Index Stock Imagery; Page 8: Visuals Unlimited/Nancy P. Alexander (top),
International Stock/Bill Stanton (bottom); Page 9: Visuals Unlimited/Jeff Greenberg; Page 10:
International Stock/Keith Wood; Page 11: International Stock/Elliott Smith; Page 12: Unicorn
Stock Photos/Tom McCarthy; Page 13: Index Stock Imagery; Page 14: Photo
Network/Bachmann; Page 15: Unicorn Stock Photos/ChromoSohm/Sohm (top),
Bachmann/Pictor (bottom); Page 16: International Stock/Scott Barrow

1 2 3 4 5 6 06 05 04 03 02 01

PEOPLE WORK

BY DEBBIE ECKER

Consulting Editor: Gail Saunders-Smith, Ph.D.
Consultants: Claudine Jellison and
Patricia Williams, Reading Recovery Teachers
Content Consultant: Andrew Gyory, Ph.D., American History

Yellow Umbrella Books

an imprint of Capstone Press
Mankato, Minnesota

Many people enjoy working.
Most people get paid
for the work they do.
People use the money to buy
things they need, such as
a home, food, and clothes.

People use money to buy
fun things they want too.

Some people work
as sales people.
They help us buy things.

Some people work as farmers.
Farmers grow food
and take care of animals.

Some people work
as forest rangers.
Forest rangers take care of the
land in a
forest.
They help
people who
visit forests
stay safe.

Some people work
as veterinarians.
Veterinarians are doctors
who take care of animals.

Some people work as teachers.
Teachers help students learn.

People work as coaches.
Some coaches help people
learn how to play sports.

And some people work
as artists.
Some artists paint.
Other artists make things.

People work as carpenters.
Carpenters work with wood
to build houses.

Some people work as plumbers.
Plumbers put in pipes
that carry water.
They fix broken pipes too.

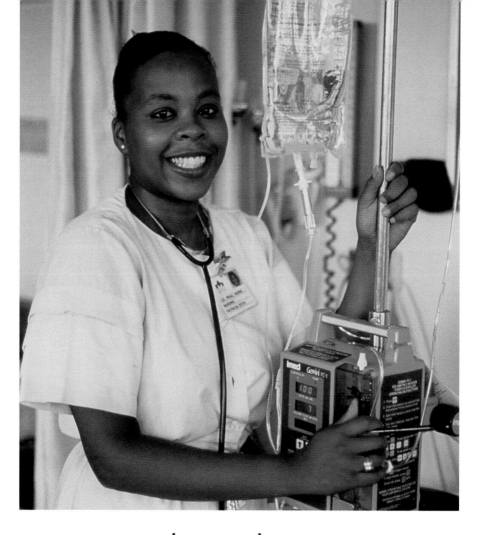

Some people work as nurses.
Nurses take care of people
who are sick or hurt.

Some people work
with computers.
Some people build
and fix computers.

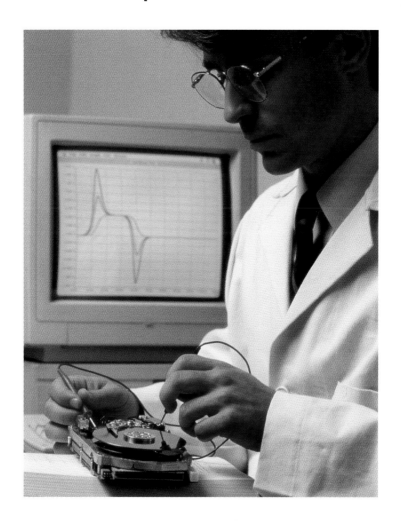

Some people work as cooks.
Cooks make food
for people to eat.

People work in factories.
They use parts to build things.

People work as postal workers.
Postal workers pick up
and drop off mail.

What kind of work would you like to do?

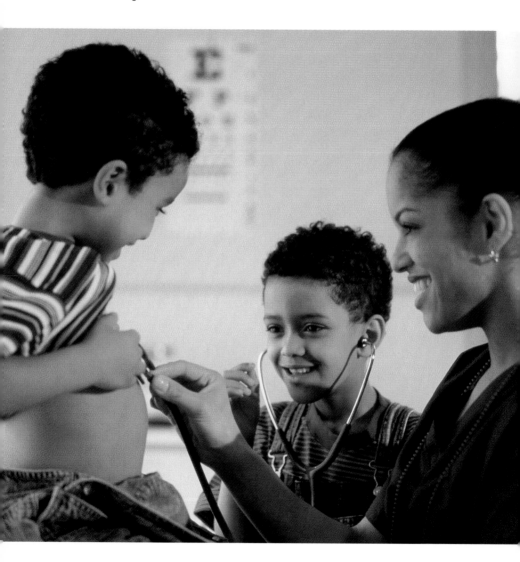

Words to Know/Index

Word Count: 233
Early-Intervention Levels: 13–16